RARE CARPETS
FROM EAST AND WEST

With an introduction by Mercedes Viale Ferrero

**ORBIS BOOKS
LONDON**

Contents

Acknowledgments are due to the following for photographs used in this volume:
Bianconi: 19
Buscaglia: 37
C. Ciccione: 2, 4, 46–50
Da Re: 36
Ferruzzi: 17, 18, 30
Freeman: 11
Giovetti: 42, 43, 53, 57, 59, 60, 63–65, 68, 69, 71, 73, 77
Gulbenkian Foundation: 3
Istituto Geografico De Agostini: 1, 5, 7, 12, 13, 15, 20–22, 24–28, 31–33, 35, 39, 40, 45, 52, 54, 56, 58, 61, 62, 66, 67, 70, 72, 74–76, 78, 79
Magnum: 41
Metropolitan Museum of Art, Hewitt Fund: 9
Metropolitan Museum of Art, Gift of Samuel H. Kress Foundation: 10
Meyer: 16
National Museum of Helsinki: 55
R. Pedicini: 29
Scala: 6, 8, 23, 38
SEF: 51
Victoria and Albert Museum: 10, 44

Translated from the Italian of Mercedes Viale Ferrero

A carpet is not simply an article to serve practical and decorative purposes; it is a true work of art which can be of the highest quality. The history of the carpet is a fascinating one, and as it is linked with the diverse arts and events of many civilisations, it is both complex and wide ranging; it has been the subject of innumerable essays, treatises and critical studies, yet the subject is by no means exhausted and there are still some aspects that require clarification.

Of course we do not pretend to be able to retrace the whole complex history of the carpet in this small volume. We shall limit ourselves to describing in words and pictures some important aspects of the art of carpet-making from the fifteenth to the eighteenth century, and then provide examples of nineteenth- and twentieth-century carpets which can easily be found on sale.

We hope that the illustrations, notes and introductory text will stimulate the reader into broadening his knowledge of carpets. To this end we have added a bibliography indicating some basic reading matter, which will give a solid historical and critical perspective to anyone who wishes to deepen his understanding of the subject.

The enthusiast will be able to complement his learning by seeing actual examples of the art of carpet-making, most of which are preserved in museums and collections open to the public and therefore easily accessible.

Anyone interested in carpets should certainly try to visit the Victoria and Albert Museum, the Mayorcas Collection, the Vigo Art Galleries and the C. John Collection (the latter two are well-known dealers) in London, and when abroad, magnificent collections can be seen at the Poldi Pezzoli Museum in Milan, the Bargello, Bardini and Argenti Museums in Florence, the San Marco Museum in Venice; in Vienna there is the Austrian Museum for Applied Arts, and in spite of a disastrous fire in 1945 there is still a notable collection at the Berlin State Museum. In France, spectacularly beautiful examples are preserved, notably in the Musée des Arts Décoratifs and the Musée des Gobelins in Paris, although there are also excellent collections elsewhere. Several museums in the United States show carpets of great value, but perhaps the richest and most comprehensive collection is housed in the Metropolitan Museum of Art in New York. Essential to the study of ancient Anatolian carpets is the Turk-Islam Museum in Istanbul.

Naturally these are just general indications. One can still experience the joy of discovering a beautiful old carpet preserved in a little museum in some provincial market-town. As his knowledge increases, the enthusiast will become an expert, able to pick out a good carpet which will adorn and enliven his home.

Mercedes Viale Ferrero

Origins and techniques

A carpet is usually defined as a fairly substantial fabric with designs and colours woven into it, and for use mainly as a floor-covering. As an item of home furnishing it certainly originated in the East, but exactly when, no one can say with any great accuracy. In the writings of classical authors there are often passages extolling the beauty of luxurious fabrics adorning the palaces of Eastern kings, but today nothing remains of those ancient works of art. The earliest hand-knotted carpet in existence was discovered by the Russian archeologist Rudenko in southern Siberia, and is at present exhibited at the Hermitage Museum, Leningrad. This carpet, known as the 'Pazyryk' was almost certainly made during the fifth century BC, but whether it was made in Persia, East Turkestan or Anatolia (Asia Minor) is still the subject of controversy. Later examples, found during excavations in East Turkestan and in Egypt, and dating from the third to the ninth century AD, are simply torn fragments from which it is difficult to obtain any clear indications. One can, however, deduce from this scanty evidence that the carpet was used by the nomad tribes of Central Asia. Certainly the carpet was – and still is – an item of furnishing very well suited to the life the nomad herdsmen lived: abundant and readily available raw materials (wool), a soft and warm finished article that was easily transportable, long-lasting and had a pleasing decorative effect. Even the earliest fragments we know (and the Pazyryk) were made with the knotting technique, that is, the design was made by using threads of wool in various colours, knotted into the woven foundation.

These are various kinds of knots, of which the two main ones are the Sehna (also called Persian) knot, and the Ghiordes (or Turkish) knot. The type of knot used does not indicate any difference in style and, on its own, does not give any sure indication of the origin of the carpet. There do exist Persian carpets with Turkish knots. The knots can be in different densities: the medallion and animal patterned carpet at the Bargello Museum in Florence (plate 6) has 10,800 Sehna knots per square decimetre (about 700 per square inch), and the bird-patterned one in the same museum (plate 39) has only 900 Ghiordes knots per square decimetre (58 per square inch). In Persia there were even (and are still) some carpets made without any knots at all; instead they are woven like tapestries (plates 19 and 20).

On the other hand Western carpet-makers have used a fairly wide variety of techniques: the Spanish knot, the Savonnerie knot, weaving without a pile in the manner of tapestries (plate 51), *petit point* embroidery (plate 54).

ORIENTAL CARPETS
PERSIA

Despite the fact that the oldest carpets now in existence are not Persian (ignoring the controversial Pazyryk), there must have been carpet-makers active in Persia in very remote times. Timurid and Mongol miniatures from the fourteenth and fifteenth centuries show carpets with stylistic characteristics quite different from the Anatolian ones. In addition, the perfection of design and technique in the earliest Persian carpets still in existence, indicates that there had already been a long tradition in carpet-making.

Towards the end of the fifteenth century and continuing through the sixteenth, there was an amazing flowering of the art of carpet-making in Persia. Shapes and styles were re-worked to produce masterpieces of peerless splendour and richness of invention, inspired composition and purity of design. It was no coincidence that this happened at a particularly favourable time in Persia's history: after having been ruled by the Seljuk dynasties and then by the Mongols, at last under Ismail I (1502–24) Persia became united and its own Safavid dynasty gained power. This sparked off a period of political, economic and artistic rebirth, and so it is not surprising that in this favourable

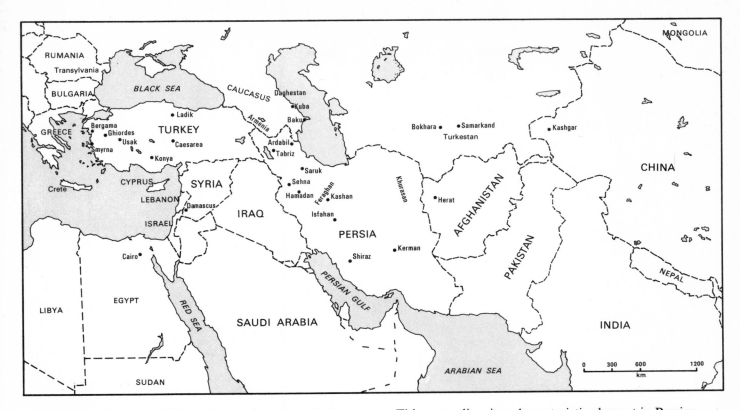

atmosphere there should be such creative energy in the art of carpet-making. On the one hand the pomp and magnificence of the new kings and their court acted as a stimulus to the manufacture of carpets, and on the other hand the carpet-makers could draw on themes and images from the wide range of contemporary Persian art, which had by then reached a very high level.

The Persian carpet did not, however, limit itself to borrowing decorative themes – such as the 'medallion' design which is the most typical – from the other artistic disciplines; it also made use of excellent miniaturists who supplied the cartoons, and even poets who composed the texts for the ornamental inscriptions. In this way the carpet became the expression of a complex range of decorative elements, iconographic values and artistic concepts, all culminating in superb works of art of great originality. The people who designed and made these carpets were so well aware of the value of their handiwork that they often signed and dated them (plates 11, 13), while poets exhalted their beauty. An example of this is a little poem inserted into the medallion carpet in the Poldi Pezzoli Museum (plate 12) which reads as follows: 'This is not a carpet, it is a white rose . . . No, it is more, it is a garden filled with lilies and roses; its beauty draws the nightingales here to sing. Look at the cascades of water that spring from its weave on every side, this is the way to the spring of youth . . . Nowhere is there a single flaw in this perfect grace . . . Oh God, this pure rose is the flawless child of the garden of hope.' The dual inspiration – naturalistic and symbolical – which had informed the designers of these carpets and been applied with harmonious coherence of style, could not have been better expressed. It is an appropriate and well-merited tribute from one artist to other artists.

This naturalism is a characteristic element in Persian art, but in carpet-making it is always contained within a disciplined framework of very carefully worked-out patterns and compositions (plates 2, 11, 14). This can be seen in carpets designed for everyday use, in which animals and even people appear, and also in prayer rugs for mosques, in which the design is made up of arabesques and plant shapes, and emblems such as the chandelier of the mosque and the pillars of wisdom.

Apart from a few fragments which probably date back to the end of the fifteenth century, the earliest undisputedly Persian carpets to have survived to the present day were made in the first half of the sixteenth century. The first known carpet actually to bear a date is the one called 'medallion and hunting scene carpet' in the Poldi Pezzoli Museum, dated 1522–3 and therefore even older than the splendid 'medallion' carpet from the Ardebil Mosque treasury, now housed in the Victoria and Albert Museum, which bears the date 1539 (plates 11, 13). Of course these dates are written according to the Mohammedan calendar, in which a year has a different length from ours and starts from Egira (15 June in the year 622 AD); for example, our year 1539 corresponds to the year 946 in the Mohammedan calendar.

It is not always easy to tell which carpets were made in which regions of Persia. However, it is believed that a certain group of carpets that are outstanding for their artistic qualities and precious materials (they are made of the finest wool, silk and silver thread) come from Tabriz. For a certain length of time, this town in northern Persia was its capital city, and the Sefavids had their court here. Other centres of carpet production were Kashan in central Persia, Kerman and Herat (now in Afghanistan) in eastern Persia.

5

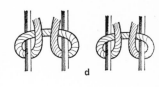

a) The Sehna (or Persian) knot.
b) Diagram showing how the Sehna knot is made.
c) The Ghiordes (or Turkish) knot.
d) Diagram showing how the Ghiordes knot is made.

Persian carpets are usually classified according to their patterns. This purely empirical approach is not wholly satisfactory, but it is useful as a point of departure.

Medallion carpets

The medallion is a very ancient design which was already present in Sassanian ceramics and materials, then used on book bindings and illuminated manuscripts (including the Koran cover), and finally transferred to the carpet, where it became a basic element in the design. There can be one central medallion surrounded by arabesques and ornate plants, sometimes embellished with pendants (plates 2, 3, 11, 14); or medallions can be distributed over the field (plate 10). Although this motif often occurs in Persian carpets, it never becomes monotonous because the shape of the medallion changes, and the swirling patterns surrounding it are of an amazing complexity; the colours are varied and their harmonies and contrasts most carefully planned.

Animal and hunting scenes

These two types are closely linked. Within the pattern of arabesques, vine tendrils and symbolical ribbons, there appear domestic and wild animals. Sometimes there are also hunters following their prey (plates 4, 5, 6, 13); these designs are particularly interesting historically because they represent, though in an idealised fashion, life at court in those times. Hunting was, in fact, the favourite sport of Persian princes and nobles.

Tree and garden carpets

These two types are also very similar to each other. Trees can be used as a decorative pattern, or else they can be laid out in an ordered manner reminiscent of a conventional representation of a garden (plate 1). In some examples they are combined with the medallion motif and sometimes even with hunting scenes (plate 4).

Vase carpets

From a central motif there extend palmettes and flowers. These carpets are almost always long and narrow. It would appear that they were reserved for use in court and mosque.

Mosaic carpets

The field is divided into several more or less irregular panels, giving an effect similar to that of a mosaic floor. The border, on the other hand, has the usual pattern of arabesques, flowers, leafy tendrils and ribbons (plate 9).

Flower and ribbon carpets

These are also called Herat carpets, after the town in which most of them were made. Palmettes and large flowers, joined by symbolic ribbons (*Tsci*), make up a close-set design. This type originated in the second quarter of the sixteenth century, continued through the seventeenth century and is still sometimes used today (plates 7, 8).

Prayer rugs

At the centre of these is the Mihrab, a sort of 'prayer-niche', the shape of which derives from the altars of mosques. This type of design is not found very often among Persian carpets (plate 23).

Besides the centres of production and the types of carpet already mentioned, several more came to prominence in the last quarter of the sixteenth century. In particular, Shah Abbas I the Great (1588–1629) established court workshops in Isfahan, the town he made capital of Persia. From these workshops came carpets of great subtlety and refinement, both in the materials used (silk and precious-metal thread), and in the magnificent range of colours. The designs are a discriminating combination of various traditional motifs (plates 17, 18,

Some decorative motifs used in old Persian carpets:
a) Vase b) Hunting scene c) Tree

٠	0	٦	6
١	1	٧	7
٢	2	٨	8
٣	3	٩	9
٤	4		
٥	5	ai	year

Arabic numerals with their Western counterparts. There are various ways of converting dates in the Mohammedan calendar to the Gregorian and Julian calendars, but it is simplest to use special conversion tables.

21, 22, 23). These are generally known as 'Shah Abbas carpets', though some of them are called *Polonaise* carpets because they were made for Polish noblemen, who had their coats-of-arms incorporated into the design. Many of the *Polonaise* carpets, including those bearing the arms of Sigismund III of Poland (plate 19) were made in Kashan, where carpets were woven in the manner of tapestries (plate 20).

Towards the end of the seventeenth century the general decadence in Persian art also affected carpet-making. Traditional designs were repeated diligently, but without any creative force behind them. Nevertheless, many of the 'Low School' carpets manufactured during the next 150 years or so are of considerable merit.

Carpets are still being made in Persia today. In the area around Kerman, the traditional medallion motif is still used in their manufacture. The same designs as those created by the ancient Herats are today being woven into the carpets of the Feraghan heights, and those made in the Khurasan region are fairly similar. Saruk carpets still have the traditional medallion and flower motif, while in those made around Sehna the predominant characteristic is the palmette design. Shiraz and its surrounding district produce geometric designs with stylised flowers that show a Caucasian influence. The heavy Bijar carpets are woven by the nomad tribes of Kurdistan, with designs inspired by Herat carpets, though much more stylised (plates 56–62). The Sehna knot is usually used.

INDIA

The Mughal emperors imported Persian craftsmen into India to work at the court workshops. Indian carpets made in the sixteenth and seventeenth centuries were of very high quality, and though strongly influenced by Persian art, local tastes tended to accentuate the naturalistic and figurative elements, while suppressing a too rigorous attention to composition. Cartoons for the designs were provided by highly skilled miniaturists (plate 16).

EGYPT

It has already been noted that some fragments of carpets (dating from the eighth or ninth century AD) have been found during excavations in Egypt. However, the first ones on which we have documented information date from the end of the fifteenth century. The oldest, extremely rare examples, are the so-called 'Mamelukes', the name deriving from the fact that they were probably woven in workshops at the Court of the Mamelukes. They are sometimes called 'Damascus carpets', but this name is incorrect because they were not made at Damascus but simply sold there. These carpets were decorated with a dense pattern of geometric figures, giving a kaleidoscopic effect (plate 25), but the colours were subdued and unvaried. Their production continued even after the Turkish conquest of Egypt (1518).

In the second half of the sixteenth century, the workshops of the Ottoman Court in Egypt developed a completely new decorative form consisting of large naturalistic designs of flowers and leaves, in which the influence of contemporary Persian art is evident. This elegant and very characteristic type is usually called 'Turkish court carpet', and its manufacture continued right through to the seventeenth century.

A later and coarser derivation from the Mameluke carpet is the so-called 'Siriac', the pattern of which is composed of squares, each one containing lozenges embellished with a variety of star, flower and tree motifs. A few were made in the sixteenth century but the majority belong to the seventeenth century. The Sehna knot still figures in them.

ASIA MINOR

At the time of the Seljuk dynasty, Turks from the vast regions of Central Asia settled in Asia Minor and other parts of the Near East. The earliest group of carpets to survive to the present day in complete, rather than fragmentary form all come from Asia Minor. This

7

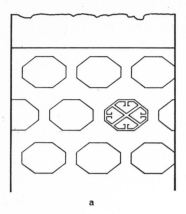

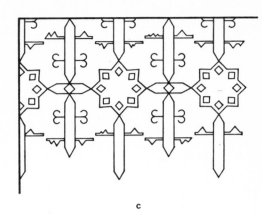

a   b   c

Some decorative motifs used in carpets found in the Ala-ed-Din Mosque in Konya (thirteenth or fourteenth century).
a) General pattern showing the decoration of one motif in a carpet with an octagonal repeating pattern.
b) Carpet design comprised of geometric shapes.
c) Diagram illustrating the design of carpet decorated with star shapes.

collection, made for the Ala-ed-Din Mosque at Konya which was built in 1220, is now kept at the Turk-Islam Museum in Istanbul, and is probably the work of the Seljuk court weavers in Konya. Experts have been unsure as to the exact date of the carpets, some attributing them to the thirteenth century and others to the fourteenth century at the latest. They are already knotted in the typical Ghiordes manner and have a simple pattern of geometric or stylised shapes on a plain field.

There is fairly complete documentation on carpets manufactured in Asia Minor. Marco Polo, for example, on visiting the towns of Konya and Caesarea in about 1271, declared that: 'here they make the most perfect carpets in the world, woven in exquisite colours.' However he did not describe them in detail, and so we do not know whether the carpets referred to were from Konya or not. Other patterns certainly did exist, and we know of a type with its field divided into squares in which geometric shapes figure. While there are no actual examples of these carpets still in existence, they do appear in various paintings and works of art such as the fresco entitled *The Dream of Pope Gregory IX* in the Upper Church at Assisi, painted by Giotto or one of his pupils in 1297. Another type had the field divided into several sections in the centre of which was a stylised figure of an animal, or sometimes two animals facing each other. An example of this type of carpet appears in *St Louis of Toulouse* (plate 29) painted by Simone Martini in 1317, and housed by the Capodimonte Museum at Naples. Anatolian carpets bearing stylised animals face-to-face were reproduced in numerous fourteenth- and fifteenth-century paintings, but it seems that after this period the animal pattern was no longer used in Asia Minor, though it was taken up in the Caucasus where it continued for some time.

It is for this reason that the only two Anatolian carpets still in existence in which the animal design is used, are thought to be fairly early fifteenth-century examples. One, now in the Berlin State Museum, comes from an unidentified church in Rome (plate 27) and the other, on show at the Stockholm Historical Museum, was found in a church in a little Swedish town called Marby (plate 28). It is significant that such rare specimens were found in two places so far apart from each other, because it leads one to assume that this type of carpet was widely used throughout Europe. It is particularly unusual to find such an old specimen in Sweden, whereas such an occurrence is not unusual for a country like Italy, since Venice and Florence were centres of trade between Europe and the Near East. Finally, it is worth noting that the design featuring in the Berlin Museum carpet (the battle between the dragon and the phoenix), was later faithfully reproduced by Taddeo di Bartolo in his fresco *Marriage of two orphans*, painted in the Hospital of Siena in 1440 or shortly after.

'Holbein' carpets

As we have already seen, the animal design fell into disuse at the end of the fifteenth century and was replaced by purely geometric shapes. Carpets using this later design are generally called 'Holbein' carpets, because Hans Holbein the Younger (1497–1543) reproduced them several times in his paintings (plate 32). This appellation is really incorrect, because such carpets had been in use long before Holbein was born, and several other painters had already incorporated them into their paintings.

It is the numerous paintings in which this particular type of carpet appears that furnish us with a clear history of its development, because the paintings can all be dated with considerable accuracy. The design, certainly an old one because it already appeared in paintings executed in the first half of the fifteenth century, shows a field divided into large sections containing geometric shapes, usually with a star-shaped outline (plate 31). Surviving carpets of this type are so rare that they can be counted on the fingers of one hand. A second design, very similar to the first, was also reproduced in fifteenth-century paintings, and has as its principal motif a star within an octagon, round which elegant ribbon shapes intertwine.

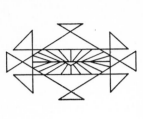
a

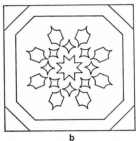
b

c

d

In these 'Holbein' carpets, the rigorously formal design does not in any way diminish their lively attractiveness. The colours are strong and luminous, and great inventiveness is shown in the extremely complex variations, when repeating motifs are used in ever-changing new arrangements. The technique of their execution is similarly excellent. However, as time passed (at the end of the sixteenth century and, in some cases, the beginning of the seventeenth century) they began to lose a certain amount of their clarity of colour and stylistic discipline, though the traditional patterns remained the same.

There is a third type of carpet which is sometimes given the 'Holbein' label: it has the same geometric pattern, but it is characterised by a series of small octagons containing a lozenge and palmette design. There are many examples of sixteenth- and seventeenth-century paintings in which this type of carpet figures, and the considerable number still surviving indicates that they must have been widely distributed throughout the world (plates 33, 34, 35, 36). These carpets have a most pleasing effect due, above all, to the wide range of lively colours on a plain red background.

Even though it is not difficult to follow the development of the various kinds of geometric-design carpets, their exact historical, stylistic and geographical origin is still problematical. For example, there is much uncertainty as to exactly what connection they have with the ancient Seljuk carpets, and we do not know with any precision where they were made, though in view of the fact that such great quantities were exported, it would be reasonable to suppose that they were made in several workshops. What we do know, however, is that the most important centres of production were Usak and Bergama.

Medallion and star carpets

Carpets with decorative themes derived from contemporary Persian examples are usually attributed to workshops at Usak. These Persian motifs are interpreted through the geometric, stylised and abstract shapes so often found in the carpets of Asia Minor.

The medallion theme was already known by the turn of the sixteenth century. Pictorial works of the time (plate 30) reproduce carpets bearing a central motif in strong relief, a design which can also be found in carpets still in existence (plate 37). As the sixteenth century advanced, this basic medallion design became rather more complex, and though still very schematic, the stylised figures took on a softer outline.

From the medallion theme grew the star shape. This is scattered, more or less densely, over a field that is usually dark red. Its shape was already well defined by the mid sixteenth century and it persisted throughout the seventeenth century (plate 38).

Prayer rugs

The religious precepts of Islam were very strictly observed in Asia Minor, and this explains the wide diffusion (which never happened in Persia) of prayer rugs bearing the usual Mihrab.

It is possible that the earliest prayer rugs absorbed influences from the Usak workshops. A later type (from the beginning of the seventeenth century until midway through the eighteenth century) is called Siebenbürgen or Transylvanian, after the region in which it was sold or found in large quantities. There is considerable variety in the design, but it always contains flowers and curving plants, sometimes highly stylised and other times executed with great realism. The Mihrab prayer-niche is double, that is, it appears at both the short ends of the carpet. This characteristic is also found in Bergama carpets, and indeed some experts have attributed the entire Transylvanian group to Bergama workshops.

New kinds of prayer rugs appeared in the seventeenth and eighteenth centuries. Those from the workshops of Ghiordes are distinguished by lively flourishes of plant shapes, probably derived from the so-called 'Turkish court carpet' (see EGYPT). Those from Melas, Kula and

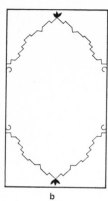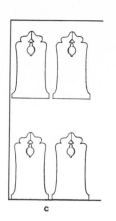

Diagrams of Mihrab rugs: a) Traditional Usak rug; b) Siebenbürgen; c) 'Family' rug.

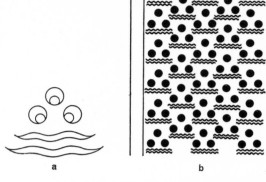

The so-called 'thunder and lightning' theme: a) Decorative motif; b) Diagram showing the arrangement of this motif over the field.

Ladik are also highly valued; the latter can be recognised by their typical Rhodes lily pattern (plate 43). There is yet another very special kind called 'the family carpet', on which the Mihrab is repeated as many times as there are members of the family to kneel on it for prayer.

Other decorative themes

There are still further varieties of Anatolian carpets: the 'thunder and lightning' theme, which is purely symbolical and has caused much controversy as to its interpretation, and the 'bird' theme, which is really a pattern of stylised leaves (plates 39, 40). These two were made from the end of the sixteenth century until the eighteenth century and have in common a white or very pale background. A later type of carpet (eighteenth century) with a large, naturalistic design inspired by the Persian style, is attributable to Smyrna workshops, which undertook commissions from European buyers (plate 42).

Fairly old specimens still came up for sale: Ghiordes, Ladiks, Bergamas, Kulas, Smyrnas and Kirsehirs (among the latter is the Mihrab decorated with stylised trees) from the nineteenth, indeed even the eighteenth century. However, the more recent production is very uneven in quality. There is a government-sponsored carpet industry at Hereke, while craftsmen still make prayer rugs at Ladik (plates 63–7). The Ghiordes knot is still used in carpets from Asia Minor.

THE CAUCASUS

A very curious phenomenon in Caucasian carpets is that some of them have designs characteristic of Anatolian workmanship in the fourteenth and fifteenth centuries, and later abandoned. The ancient dragon and phoenix pattern (plate 27) and facing animals separated by a tree (plate 28) were revived by Caucasian craftsmen, who incorporated them into new decorative themes consisting of flowers, leaves and palmettes of Persian origin. The final product is very opulent, with a certain formality of design; it has great individuality and is quite distinct from the Anatolian and Persian types. There is much controversy as to the dating of these Caucasian 'dragon' carpets (though several other kinds of animals also appear in them) because they were made over a long period of time. It is possible that the oldest examples (the one displayed in the State Museum of Berlin and seriously damaged during the last war, and perhaps also the one kept at the Victoria and Albert Museum in London) date from the sixteenth century. The rest can be variously assigned to the seventeenth (plate 44) and eighteenth centuries. The 'dragon' carpets are sometimes also called 'Armenian' by those experts who believe they were made in Armenia. As this region borders with the Caucasus, it is highly probable that ideas and influences would have crossed the border in both directions.

Another type of carpet from Caucasus is the 'flower' or 'tree and flower' kind, probably originating in the seventeenth or eighteenth century and inspired by Persian motifs. Carpets with a highly stylised pattern of large flowers alternating with rosettes are also attributable to the Caucasus. The Ghiordes knot appears here too.

One of the more noticeable characteristics of Caucasian carpets is the coarse weave, perhaps a reflection on the comparative poverty of the region. Many of these carpets have fewer than 80 knots per square inch.

A strong tendency to stylisation of ornamental themes characterises the nineteenth- and twentieth-century Caucasian carpets now on sale. From the region around the town of Baku come the Kuba carpets (with a flower, palmette and star design), the Hilas (with a small traditional medallion design) and the Shirvans (a coarser type of weave with its decoration including roughly sketched-in animal figures). In north-west Daghestan one can find the 'chichi' type with a rosette design, and in the southern Caucasus the Kazakhs with powerful geometrical ornamentation and lively colours (plates 68–71, 73). Sumak carpets are not knotted but are woven like tapestries, with a design consisting of octagons and stars (plate 72).

10

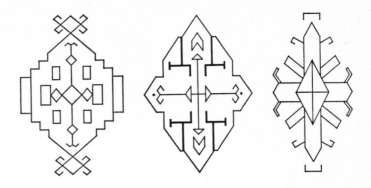

Some decorative motifs found in carpets from Central Asia.

CENTRAL ASIA

The art of carpet-making probably had its distant origins in the vast regions of Turkestan. However, existing carpets that can be positively identified as Turkmen are comparatively recent, no earlier than nineteenth century. Their decoration is mainly geometrical, with a few elements that may have a distant connection with the old Anatolian designs, though they are very simplified and of much lower quality.

The most common motif, the so-called 'elephant's foot' or 'gul', is an octagon divided into four parts by a cross. These octagons are usually distributed over the field in regular rows. Turkmen carpets are usually classified on a tribal basis: the finely-woven Tekke carpets; the Beshir, with stylised flowers inserted between the usual octagons; and the Yomud, in which the octagons are shaped in the special 'hooked diamond' style. Afghan rugs, with a similar design but more roughly made, are also classified as Turkmen, though of course they come from Afghanistan (plates 74–7).

Carpets from Chinese Turkestan have very particular characteristics, and there are examples dating back to the eighteenth century. Their decoration makes use of many themes from Chinese art, such as the Lotus, the Pomegranate, the Peony and symbolical Clouds. The most outstanding examples come from Kashgar and Kotan, although they are sometimes referred to as Samarkand, after the ancient Turkmen capital (plates 78, 79).

CHINA

Chinese carpets (which come from the northern provinces) are quite different from other Oriental types. The designs are symbols (Buddhist and Taoist) and they are freely scattered over the field, with a lively pictorial skill. The colours are delicate, with blue and yellow prevailing (plate 45). Although some very rare examples can be traced back to the seventeenth century, most belong to the eighteenth and nineteenth centuries.

SPAIN

Although the earliest Spanish carpets belong to the Islamic era, they have been included under the heading of European carpets, for ease of geographic classification.

EUROPEAN CARPETS

No sensible comparison can be made between Oriental and Western carpets because they are two completely different modes of expression. The reason for this is not so much a matter of technique, but rather that ideas about what constitutes a decorative effect are basically different, and have been different for a very long time. Towards the end of the twelfth century, a most unusual woman with a sound knowledge of literature, art and politics, decided to embark upon the making of a knotted carpet. The woman was Agnes, abbess at a convent in Quedlinburg, and with the help of her nuns the carpet was completed in 1203.

Although the 'Spanish' knot used in its making originated in the East, this work – still preserved in the Cathedral of Quedlinburg – bears no resemblance at all to Oriental carpets. It is a 'pictorial' representation of *The Marriage of Mercury and Philology*, inspired by the writings of Martianus Capella (fifth century AD), and the carpet has figures reminiscent of those in Romanesque paintings.

The work of this abbess did not have any immediate followers, but it does demonstrate that examples of knotted carpets made in the East and in Spain, must have been known in Central Europe from the twelfth century.

11

Drawings of two of the figures woven into the famous 'Quedlinburg carpet'.

SPAIN

The Arabs began the conquest of the Iberian peninsula in the year 710. For long the Spanish opposed them in vain, but finally in the twelfth and thirteenth centuries the Moslem power began to decline steadily, although it was not broken completely until the fall of Granada in 1492. It is not surprising, therefore, that the earliest carpets made in Spain have many qualities in common with Anatolian carpets. Nevertheless, they can be differentiated by noting the variations in technique. The Spanish knot is a single-warp knot twisted on to a single-warp thread.

There is documentary evidence of the existence of a number of carpet workshops in Spain dating as far back as the twelfth and thirteenth centuries. New decorative themes appeared in the sixteenth century: the so-called 'Mudejar' carpets with patterns taken from contemporary woven materials (plate 52), and carpets with heraldic arms and emblems superimposed on an ornately patterned field (plate 53). In the sixteenth and seventeenth centuries the main centres of production were Cuenca and Alcazar, and in the eighteenth century 'The Royal Manufacturers of Tapestries and Carpets' was instituted at Madrid; they cut loose from local traditions and accepted new developments dictated by European tastes in the decorative arts. Alpujarras carpets, which have been produced in southern Spain during the nineteenth and twentieth centuries, are good examples of the work done by local artisans.

FRANCE

The initial stimulus to carpet-making in France was economic. At the beginning of the seventeenth century, such vast numbers of Oriental carpets were imported into France as to have an adverse effect on the economy. Therefore, when an artisan called Pierre Dupont declared that he could 'make carpets with a pile in the manner of the Eastern masters', Henry IV of France decided to encourage his initiative by giving his permission to open his own workshop at the Louvre (1606). In actual fact the technique Dupont used was not exactly the same as that used in Oriental carpets, but the results were good, so good, that a pupil of his, Simon Lourdet, opened his own workshop in 1627. Lourdet established this workshop in a building that had formerly been used for the making of soap – hence the name Savonnerie, which means 'soap-makers'. The Louvre and Savonnerie industries worked in conjunction with each other, and in 1672 combined under the same roof (the Savonnerie). Then in 1712 'The Royal Furniture-makers and Weavers of Carpets in the Persian and Oriental Manner' was founded, and in 1826 it was amalgamated with the Gobelin industry, an association maintained to this day.

The early Savonnerie and Louvre carpets, with their floral patterns and (occasionally) figures and landscapes on a dark background, do not at all resemble the Oriental carpets Dupont first set out to imitate (plate 46). They resemble much more the tapestries – especially the *menues verdures* variety – and furniture coverings of their time. This similarity seems to indicate a desire to integrate the carpet into their own decorative environment, to form a coherent whole.

Beginning in 1672, Charles Le Brun designed the carpets for the magnificent palaces of Louis XIV of France (plate 47). Le Brun's carpets, much in the manner of classic French painting, were designed to harmonise with the surrounding decor and furnishings. Motifs appearing in his carpets are often identical to those decorating the ceiling above them; this was a typically seventeenth-century device, whereby an illusion of infinite continuity of space was created by mirror-like repetitions of surfaces. Of course, patterns were not always repeated so exactly, but there was always a profound harmony between the carpet and its sculptural, architectural and pictorial surroundings.

On the other hand, these carpets lose the ability to merge with any environment, one of the fundamental characteristics of Oriental carpets. At the same time they

12

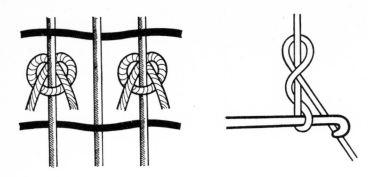

Left: diagram showing the Spanish knot. Right: the Savonnerie knot. The wool used to give the carpet its pattern is knotted around a hook at one end. All the loops are cut together, line by line, instead of being cut after each knot as in Oriental carpets.

lose the priceless advantage of being adaptable to other modes of artistic expression (plates 26, 29–32, 35, 36, 41). Le Brun's approach to carpet design spread throughout France, and indeed throughout all Europe.

It is natural that as tastes changed, so did the designs used for carpets. The solemn tones of Le Brun gave way to the softer and more universally pleasing rococo designs: thus Savonnerie carpets adopted the flowers, flourishes and tendrils dictated by an artificial conception of nature. However, the substitution of one style for the other was a very slow process, because once a model had been created it was reproduced for several years. Le Brun was succeeded by the designer Belin de Fontenay in 1687, who was in turn succeeded by his son in 1715. Then from 1715 to 1749 Pierre Josse Perrot (plate 48) worked in conjunction with Belin de Fontenay the Younger, and from 1750 till 1760 the designs were provided by Chevillon, a pupil of Perrot's. Later, Maurice Jacques introduced the 'Greek' style into carpet design; this style was inspired by a rather loose form of classicism, in harmony with Louis XVI decorations and furniture. Nevertheless, even at this late date, the old designs of Charles Le Brun and Pierre Perrot were still being used in the Savonnerie workshops. This rather conservative attitude was not overcome till the beginning of the nineteenth century, when Percier, Fontaine and Saint-Ange introduced their designs (plate 50).

Besides making ordinary carpets, the Savonnerie craftsmen also produced original works of art (imitating paintings) to be hung on walls. These extravagant objects became particularly fashionable during the reign of Louis XVI, although they had been made from the earliest days of the Savonnerie (usually as presents for the very influential).

Aubusson

The Savonnerie worked almost exclusively for the royal family and their court, whereas the group of artisans who established themselves at Aubusson worked for the

general public. This meant that prices could not be too high, and that the work had to be carried out quickly in order to satisfy as many customers as possible. Most Aubusson carpets were tapestry-woven for these very reasons. This method had the advantages of not requiring any additional equipment, as it employed the same low-heddle looms which were already familiar to the tapestry-weavers, and of using less wool than would have been required for knotted carpets. Another considerable advantage was that with this method the design was much clearer in outline. This doubtless explains the extraordinary success of the 'smooth carpets' of Aubusson which, starting in the eighteenth century, continued to be extremely fashionable right through the nineteenth century. The name of Aubusson is today often applied to 'smooth carpets' in general, whether they were made in the town of Aubusson or not.

Some knotted carpets were also made at Aubusson, using the *point de Savonnerie* (plate 49), and while they were not of the same fine quality and sumptuous design as the ones made in Paris, they have a most pleasing effect and are quite valuable. Finally, carpets of rather lesser quality were made at Felletin from the late eighteenth century onwards.

Beauvais

An effort was made to introduce the manufacture of *point de Savonnerie* knotted carpets into the town of Beauvais, where there had been a highly successful tapestry industry since the seventeenth century. However, the attempt met with little success and lasted only from 1780 till 1792, with a very brief resurgence in the middle of the next century.

ENGLAND

Some knotted carpets were made in England in the sixteenth and seventeenth centuries; these were called 'Turkey works' (the earliest carpets had been imported from Turkey) and cushion and furniture covers were also made in the same way. These early carpets are extremely rare. Then in the eighteenth century several centres of carpet production sprang up, with a quite considerable output.

Fulham

Pierre Parisot, an ex-capucine monk who had fled Lorraine, set up a carpet workshop in Fulham in 1750. He succeeded in importing workmen from Savonnerie and obtained the support of the Duke of Cumberland, but in spite of this, production ceased in 1755.

Exeter

Parisot was bought out by a rich wool merchant, Claude Passavant, who set up a carpet factory at Exeter. A very beautiful carpet, dated 1757 and now in the Victoria and Albert Museum in London, is one of the few examples of his work still in existence, and gives ample testimony to the high artistic and technical quality of these Exeter carpets. A prominent Italian gentleman, Giuseppe Baretti, visited Passavant's factory in 1760 and later described it in glowing terms. However, production ceased shortly thereafter, probably due to competition from other carpet-makers who charged lower prices.

Axminster

In the middle of the eighteenth century Thomas Whitty opened a carpet factory at Axminster. The workmanship was good and the prices relatively low; the enterprise flourished, and production was continued by Whitty's descendants until 1835. Many Axminster carpets were commissioned by the English nobility, and a number of fine examples are still in existence, most notably some of the beautiful carpets that adorned Brighton Pavilion (constructed 1810–20). The Wilton factory, with which the Axminster factory merged, is still producing carpets.

Moorfields

Carpets from the Moorfields workshop of Thomas Moore are in many ways the most interesting examples of eighteenth-century English carpet-making. Moore worked in close collaboration with the celebrated architect, Robert Adam, and the adoption of Adam's refined classicism to carpet-design produced highly pleasing results. Several Adam designs for Moorfields are kept in the Sir John Soane's Museum, Lincoln's Inn Fields (London). Quite a few Moorfields carpets (still in beautiful condition) enrich the decor of stately homes: there is one at Syon house, dated 1769, and two at Osterley House, dated between 1775 and 1778. Moore had connections with several other important people in artistic circles besides Robert Adam: for instance, a document written in 1778 mentions his friendship with the peerless furniture-maker Chippendale, a point that is of considerable interest to students of his style.

The rapid industrialisation that overtook England at the beginning of the nineteenth century produced a climate that was not favourable to the manufacture of hand-knotted carpets. With the introduction of Jacquard mechanical looms, machine-worked carpets – usually moquettes made at Wilton, Kidderminster and other industrial centres – could be sold at prices so low as to eliminate any possible competition. In 1878, however, William Morris decided to revive the dying art; he set up his looms in Hammersmith, and then moved to Merton Abbey in 1881. Although Morris showed questionable taste in attempting to recreate an obsolete style, in striving to produce replicas of medieval craftmanship, the works themselves are valuable additions.

ITALY

Italy, and in particular Venice, was the centre of trade in Oriental carpets from the thirteenth to the seventeenth century. Perhaps it was this very situation that prevented the development of local centres of production, for what was the point in going to the trouble of making carpets when enormous profits could be made simply by selling the carpets which poured in from the East?

Even in the eighteenth century, the few carpets made in Italy were not the product of large-scale manufacturers, but of court weavers who worked on special commissions. This was the case with the Papal workshops in St Michele a Ripa, Rome, where they tried to imitate the Savonnerie style. It was also the case with the court weavers at Turin, of whose efforts only one example remains (plate 51). It is most unfortunate that all the others, made especially for the Royal Palace, are now lost, and with them any clear understanding of their decorative style.

In some regions of Italy, such as Abruzzo and above all Sardinia, a popular tradition of hand-made carpets still exists. The designs are more or less geometrical and stylised.

FINLAND

The Finnish *Ryijy* (commonly referred to as 'Ryas') are the work of local artisans. The geometric and floral designs are rooted in the most ancient tradition, a tradition virtually untouched by outside influences, despite many points of contact with the neighbouring Scandinavian countries. Ryas carpets are knotted in a special way, and were also used as covers for beds and the seats of sledges. Recently there has been an attempt to revive the craft, adapting old shapes and designs to fit in with modern tastes; very worthwhile results have been obtained.

Embroidered carpets

Since the beginning of the sixteenth century there have been embroidered carpets in Europe – using cross-stitch, herring-bone stitch, *petit point*, and always on a canvas base. Most notably in Switzerland, the designs found in Oriental carpets were imitated. A most extraordinary example of this is a carefully executed imitation 'Holbein', dated 1533 and kept in the Schweizer Landesmuseum, Zurich. These works were usually not put on the floor but used as covers for tables. Embroidered carpets enjoyed a great vogue in England in the seventeenth and eighteenth centuries, with the Oriental-type design gradually being replaced by a more Western conception, using garlands of flowers and leaves.

At the beginning of the nineteenth century carpets embroidered in *petit point* had a sudden and huge success in France (plate 54). The vogue spread to other European nations as well, but it lasted longest in England, which has a very old tradition in embroidery.

Modern carpets

It is not possible in such a small space to describe the modern carpet industry (hand-woven and machine-woven) especially since there is such variety in quality and technique. It must be sufficient to say only that highly skilled artists and designers have and are providing cartoons for well-qualified manufacturers. Their work is in harmony with the images and aspirations of modern art, and amply satisfy present-day tastes in decoration.

Bibliography

Oriental carpets
Dilley, A. U., *Oriental Rugs & Carpets*, Philadelphia–
  New York 1959.
Edwards, A. Cecil, *The Persian Carpet*, London 1953.
Haack, H., *Oriental Rugs, An Illustrated Guide*, London 1960.
Hawley, Walter A., *Oriental Rugs Antique and Modern*, New York 1913.
Pope, A. U., *A Survey of Persian Art*, Vols III and VI, Oxford 1938.

European carpets
Jarry, M., *The Carpets of the Manufacture de la Savonnerie*,
  Leigh-on-Sea 1966.
Kendrick, A. F., and Tattersall, C. E. C., *Handwoven Carpets*,
  London 1922.
Mayorcas, M. J., *English Needlework Carpets 16th to 19th Centuries*,
  Leigh-on-Sea 1963.

1

1 *Garden carpet*. North-west Persia, sixteenth century (Vienna, Austrian Museum for Applied Arts). This is the oldest existing example of the garden carpet. The design has evolved from the tree carpet and represents a garden divided into beds of flowers. The double perspective is an unusual conception: the flower beds are shown from above, the trees in profile. Metal thread has been inserted into the weft. The carpet was probably made for a local ruler.

2 *Medallion carpet.* North-west Persia, first third of the sixteenth century (Paris, Musée des Gobelins). Originally the carpet was much larger than it is now. At the centre appears the medallion, a typically Persian creation. The carpet authority, A. U. Pope has declared this to be 'a work of genius'. The arabesque pattern is made up of four different decorative themes, which intertwine with each other and form a harmonious whole, with mathematical precision in an infinitely repeating rhythm.

3 *Medallion carpet.* Probably made in Tabriz, first half of the sixteenth century (Lisbon, Gulbenkian Foundation). Around the central medallion is a double arrangement of beautifully curving arabesques. The colour is rich without being flamboyant. The carpet comes from the Austrian imperial collection and it has been said, though it cannot be proved, that it once belonged to the Emperor Charles V.

3

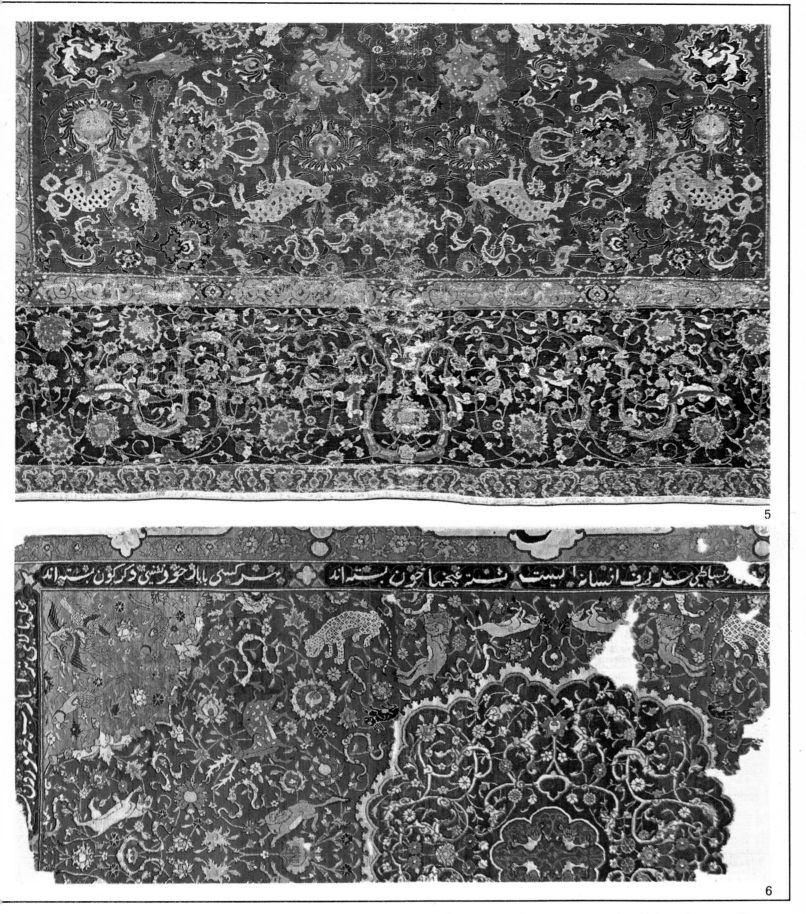

5

6

4 *Medallion and tree carpet.* Possibly made in the Karabakh workshops (in the opinion of A. U. Pope), late sixteenth century (Paris, Louvre). The carpet comes from the church of Notre Dame at Mantes. Its designer has combined the tree motif with the medallion motif, and has added figures of animals and hunters. Such complexity of design was used to obtain a luxurious effect, full of movement and colour.

5 *Flower and animal carpet.* Eastern Persia, mid sixteenth century (Vienna, Austrian Musuem for Applied Arts).

6 *Medallion, flowers and animal carpet* (fragment). Tabriz, mid sixteenth century (Florence, Bargello Museum). The previous carpet from eastern Persia and this one from western Persia show that the theme of animals on a floral background was used thoughout the country. Of course this design can vary slightly from place to place, but the style is always a strong and pictorially very effective one.

7

7 *Herat flower and ribbon carpet*. Eastern Persia, end of the sixteenth century (Milan, Poldi Pezzoli Museum).

8 *Herat flower and ribbon carpet*. Eastern Persia, early seventeenth century (Florence, Bardini Museum). In Eastern Persia the technique of decorating carpets with stylised flowers and curls of ribbons flourished for a long time. Many examples have survived to the present day, and they are known as Herat carpets, after the name of the town in which most of them were made.

9 *Mosaic carpet*. Tabriz, early sixteenth century (New York, Metropolitan Museum). This type of carpet has a rather eclectic style, combining various decorative themes to obtain a mosaic effect. Its value is not so much in the originality of design, but rather the virtuosity of composition, the brightness of the colours and the excellent quality of the weaving.

8

10

10 *Medallion and animal carpet*. Tabriz, mid sixteenth century (London, Victoria and Albert Museum). This carpet is one of a rather rare group in which several medallions are reproduced. The design bears clear traces of Chinese influence. On the whole, the composition is quite flexible, but the designer had taken particular trouble over the individual items of decoration, which are of an exquisitely delicate grace.

11 *Medallion carpet*. Kashan, 1539 (London, Victoria and Albert Museum). This carpet has the date of completion and the name of the designer (Maqsud of Kashan) woven into its pattern. It bears the old medallion motif, enlivened by a splendid profusion of floral designs surrounding it. The carpet was discovered at the Ardebil Mosque, and was probably made on the instructions of Shah Tahmasp I, who reigned from 1524 to 1567.

12

13

12 *Medallion and animal carpet.* Tabriz, approximately mid sixteenth century (Milan, Poldi Pezzoli Museum). Outstanding in this carpet is the refinement of the design, and the rich variety of themes contained in it. Between the centre panel and the wide border, is a band bearing a long inscription in verse, a full-scale poem in praise of the carpet. One of the verses reads: 'It has been woven with the thread of the soul; it had been woven for King Darius, ruler of the world.' This probably means that it was woven for Shah Tahmasp I.

13 *Medallion and hunting scene carpet.* North-west Persia, 1522–3 (Milan, Poldi Pezzoli Museum). This is in all probability the earliest Persian carpet that can be dated with certainty. It is signed by Ghiyat-ed-Din Jami and dated 929 from Egira, which corresponds to 1522–3 in our calendar. Some experts have read this figure as 949, but the very original style and expressiveness of design seem to indicate that the former date is correct.

14 *Medallion and arabesque carpet*. Tabriz, second half of the sixteenth century (New York, Metropolitan Museum). The carpet was originally in a collection owned by the Dukes of Anhalt, and is one of the few to have survived to this day in a perfect state of preservation. With great inventive skill the design combines spiralling arabesques, stylised clouds and clusters of flowers in a harmonious whole.

15

15 *Vaq-Vaq-tree carpet* (fragment). Indo-Persian border, late fifteenth or early sixteenth century (Paris, Musée des Arts Décoratifs). It is difficult to determine the exact origin of this work, as it contains both Persian and Indian decorative elements. There is no doubt, however, that the 'talking tree' or 'Vaq-Vaq' is a concept of Indian origin.

16 *Prayer rug*. India, early seventeenth century (Vienna, Austrian Museum for Applied Arts). During the Mughal dynasty magnificent carpets, outstanding for the exuberant realism of their designs, were made in India. Here, the Mihrab shape is filled with a profusion of colourful flowers, which stands out sharply in contrast with the more severe border around it.

17

18

17 *Shah Abbas medallion carpet.* Isfahan, early seventeenth century
(Venice, San Marco Basilica).

18 *Shah Abbas plant pattern carpet.* Isfahan, early seventeenth century
(Venice, San Marco Basilica). These two carpets are made with silk and
precious-metal thread, and were given by Shah Abbas I to the Doge of
Venice. Shah Abbas encouraged the production and the export of carpets,
some of which were made at the court of Isfahan, some in other parts of
Persia. An invariable characteristic of these carpets is that they are always
made with precious materials of subtle colours, woven into traditional
decorative themes.

19

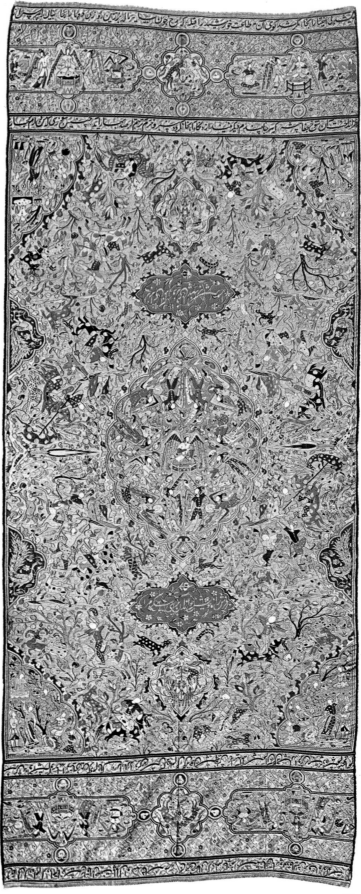

20

19 *Carpet bearing the arms of Sigismund III of Poland.* Kashan, 1602 (Munich, Residenzmuseum). In 1602 Sigismund sent his envoy to Persia with the instructions that a special carpet bearing the King's arms should be woven, and other carpets acquired as well. These latter were given as a dowry to the King's daughter, Anne Catherine Constance, when she married the Palatine Elector. They finally became the property of the Wittelsbach family. It is a characteristic of this group of carpets that rather than being knotted, they are woven like tapestries.

20 *Medallion carpet with human figures and hunting scene.* Kashan, approximately 1600 (Munich, Residenzmuseum). This very fine carpet was also tapestry-woven, and it was bought in Kashan by Muratowicz, Sigismund III's envoy. Unlike the carpet shown in plate 19, this was not specially commissioned by the King and so it does not bear his coat-of-arms.

21

21–22 *Shah Abbas plant-patterned carpet.* Isfahan, early seventeenth century (Florence, Argenti Museum).

23 *Shah Abbas prayer rug.* Persia (Kashan), early seventeenth century (Florence, Argenti Museum). All three of these carpets are of excellent quality. In particular, the prayer rug is outstanding for its elegance of design, the skill of its execution and its excellent state of preservation.

22

24 *Portuguese carpet* (so-called). Southern Persia, early seventeenth century (Vienna, Austrian Museum for Applied Arts). This extremely rare type (only about ten of them are still in existence) has been erroneously called 'Portuguese'. The mistake probably occurred because of the design at the two ends, showing a group of European travellers arriving at a port.

26

25 *Mameluke carpet,* sometimes called *Damascus carpet.* Egypt, early sixteen century (Vienna, Austrian Museum for Applied Arts). Carpets of this extremely rare type were once attributed to workshops in Damascus, though they were really made in Egypt. The example in Vienna is one of the oldest known, and it is characterised by its sober colour scheme and the great precision of the geometric designs.

26 *Turkish court carpet with plant design.* Egypt, mid sixteenth century (San Gimignano, Civic Museum). This carpet is decorated with the naturalistic patterns typical of the Turkish court style, and was made in the form of a cross for a very good reason: it was to cover a table and therefore had to have a central section with four flaps.

28

27 *Carpet showing the battle of the dragon and the phoenix.* Anatolia, early fifteenth century (Berlin, State Museum). It was purchased by Bode, the famous carpet expert, who discovered it in a church in Rome. Its date can be estimated with considerable accuracy by comparing it with the paintings in which carpets of a similar design appear; for example, exactly the same design has been reproduced in a fresco by Taddeo di Bartolo, painted between 1440 and 1444, *Marriage of two orphans* (Siena Hospital).

28 *Carpet with tree and stylised animals.* Anatolia, early fifteenth century (Stockholm, Historical Museum). It originally came from a church in Marby, Sweden. As it is so similar to the carpet in the preceding photograph, it is most likely from the same period. It could, however, date from the fourteenth century.

30

29 SIMONE MARTINI, *St Louis of Toulouse crowning Robert of Anjou*, 1317 (Naples, Capodimonte Museum).

30 VITTORE CARPACCIO, detail from *St Tryphon taming the basilisk*, 1502–8 (Venice, Schiavoni School). Such paintings provide valuable information on the history of the carpet. It is through them that we can gain knowledge about types of carpets no longer in existence, and assign fairly accurate dates to those we do still possess. In the painting by Simone Martini one can see lying at the foot of the throne, a carpet of Anatolian make, showing stylised eagles. This proves that these carpets were already known in Italy at the beginning of the fourteenth century. Also Anatolian, but of much more recent date, are the carpets painted by Carpaccio. In this, and other pictorial works of the same period, one can note the custom of hanging carpets at windows and balconies on festive occasions.

32

31 DOMENICO GHIRLANDAIO, *Madonna and child with saints and angels* (detail), about 1480 (Florence, Uffizi Gallery).

32 HANS HOLBEIN THE YOUNGER, *Portrait of George Gisze,* 1532 (Berlin, Gemäldegalerie). A certain type of carpet from Asia Minor, decorated with a geometrical design consisting mainly of squares, octagons and stars, is commonly called a 'Holbein'. It is called this after the painter Hans Holbein the Younger, who painted several such carpets in his pictures. However, this type of carpet was already widely known in the fifteenth century and appears in various paintings by Mantegna, Foppa, Carpaccio, Ghirlandaio, Lorenzo di Credi, Hans Memling and Petrus Christus.

34

33 *Geometric design carpet.* Asia Minor, second half of the sixteenth century (Florence, Bargello Museum).

34 Detail from a *Geometric design carpet* (private collection).

35 LORENZO LOTTO, *Alms from St Antonino* (detail), 1542 (Venice, Church of St John and St Paul).

36 EVARISTO BASCHENIS, *Self portrait with musician,* about 1570 (Bergamo, the Counts of Agliardi). Closely related to the 'Holbeins', these carpets have geometric designs of lozenges and palmettes, and are frequently shown in sixteenth-century paintings. They continued to be made throughout the seventeenth century, but as time went on they lost their former strength of design and structure.

37 *Medallion carpet.* Usak, early sixteenth century (Milan, Poldi Pezzoli Museum). This is one of the oldest examples of a medallion carpet still in existence, and was probably made at Usak, using the typical motif of Persian carpets. In Asia Minor, this motif became stylised into a geometrical shape, which is clearly evident in this example: the composition is severe and formal.

38 *Star carpet.* Usak, beginning of the seventeenth century (Florence, Bargello Museum). As time went on, the medallion carpets made at Usak became more varied in their design, and the star motif came into being. This carpet, now at the Bargello, originally came from the Florentine church of St Laurence of Miransù.

39

40

39 *Bird Carpet* (so-called). Asia Minor (Usak), late sixteenth century (Florence, Bargello Museum).

40 *Bird Carpet* (so-called). Asia Minor, eighteenth century (private collection). The successful and enduring 'bird' design gets its name from an incorrect interpretation of the characteristic motif, which in reality represents a stylised leaf. The oldest examples, such as the specimen at the Bargello, are of considerable dimensions and have a very clear-cut design; later (late eighteenth century) they became smaller and the design rather less precise, though the decorative effect is still very pleasing.

41 *The study of Galileo in Florence.* The widespread diffusion of Oriental carpets throughout Europe can be explained by their great versatility, as well as their artistic and decorative value. They were, of course, used to cover the floor (plates 29, 31), but they also became colourful ornaments for windows, verandas and balconies (plate 30), and made sumptuous coverings for tables (plates 26, 32, 36). Galileo's study in Florence still has the original furniture and instruments used by the great scientist. It is possible that even the carpet spread over the table was part of the original furnishings; in any case it makes an effective addition to an early seventeenth-century study.

42

43

42 *Carpet with plant decorations.* Smyrna, eighteenth century (private collection). This carpet comes from Asia Minor, probably made in Smyrna, and is a late example decorated with plant patterns of Persian origin. These are not usually works of very high quality, but their delicate colours give a pleasing effect.

43 *Prayer rug.* Ladik, eighteenth century (private collection). As already mentioned, prayer rugs – of which there are a great many throughout Asia Minor – are characterised by the Mihrab shape, which can be single or multiple, with or without decorations (among which the ritual lamp shape is the most common). The example illustrated is a rather late one, as demonstrated by the somewhat spare design, but the colours are notably beautiful. Other examples of prayer rugs are shown in plates 16, 23, 63–6.

44 *Dragon carpet,* sometimes also called *Armenian carpet.* Caucasus, early seventeenth century (London, Victoria and Albert Museum). This is a typical example of the type of Caucasian carpet distinguished by stylised dragons, and numerous other animals placed among large plant designs. These carpets are very difficult to date and are sometimes known as 'Armenian' because of the possibility that they may have originated from that country.

45

45 *Carpet with symbolical designs.* China, eighteenth century (London, Victoria and Albert Museum). This carpet, with its delicate colours, is a good example of the best in Chinese carpet-making. Note the fluid composition of the middle section and the very graceful maze design round the border.

46 *Carpet with floral and heraldic phoenix design.* Paris, Savonnerie, 1663 (Musée Jacquemart-André). The characteristic design of early Savonnerie carpets – the dark background and the exhuberant flower decorations – can be clearly seen in this example. The total effect is rather similar to the *verdures* tapestries, but production of this type did not last for long.

47

47 *Carpet bearing the coat-of-arms of Louis XIV of France.* Paris, Savonnerie, 1678 (Musée des Arts Décoratifs). This carpet was part of a collection of 93 destined for the Grand Gallery in the Louvre. The complete set of carpets was designed by Charles Le Brun, and is typical of his work: a certain eloquence of expression, harmonising perfectly with the architectural surrounds.

48 *Carpet for the Queen's bed-chamber.* Designed by Belin de Fontenay and Perrot, this carpet was woven at the Savonnerie workshops between 1728 and 1730 for Maria Leczinska, consort of Louis XV of France. After many vicissitudes the carpet at last reached the Louvre, but by then it was cut in half. In 1960–4 an exact copy was made of it at the Gobelins workshops, in order to reconstruct the original aspect of the Queen's bed-chamber at Versailles.

49

49 *Point de Savonnerie carpet.* Aubusson, mid eighteenth century (Paris, Musée Nissim-de-Camondo). Aubusson carpets were usually tapestry-woven, but some were made with the Savonnerie knotting technique.

50 *Carpet with large central motif.* Paris, Savonnerie, early nineteenth century (Malmaison). The very elegant design, incorporating classical features on a pale background, was provided by Saint-Ange.

50

51 *Tapestry-woven carpet.* Turin, 1782 (Royal Palace). Many carpets were woven in the tapestry manufactory in Turin, founded by Carlo Emanuele III of Savoy. Sadly, this is the only one to have survived. It is outstanding for the harmony and elegance of its design.

51

52

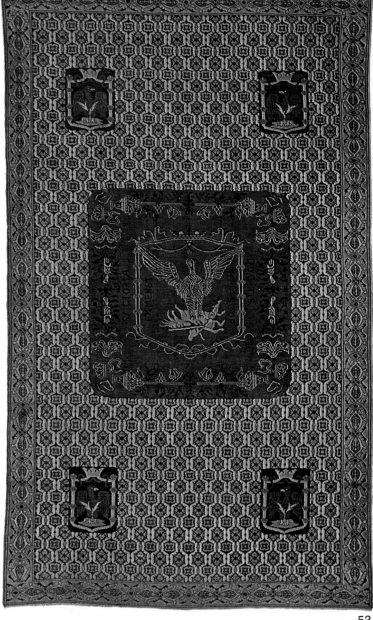

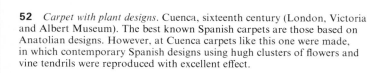

52 *Carpet with plant designs*. Cuenca, sixteenth century (London, Victoria and Albert Museum). The best known Spanish carpets are those based on Anatolian designs. However, at Cuenca carpets like this one were made, in which contemporary Spanish designs using hugh clusters of flowers and vine tendrils were reproduced with excellent effect.

53 *Heraldic design carpet*.   Spain, seventeenth century (private collection) It is by no means unusual to find Spanish carpets made in Cuenca or other centres which have heraldic motifs incorporated, more or less successfully, into the general pattern.

54

54 *Flower and bird carpet.* France, nineteenth century. The use of *petit point* embroidery in carpets is certainly not a recent idea: it has been employed since the sixteenth century. But suddenly in the early nineteenth century it gained extraordinary popularity and widespread use. This little carpet has a certain ingenuous grace, which is common to many other examples of the same type.

55 *Ryas carpet,* dated 1782, Finland (Helsinki, National Museum). The Finnish Ryas (or *Ryijy*) are small carpets of very ancient origin. It was the custom that every girl should make one for her trousseau. The type of decoration is quite varied, but it usually employs as a basis the geometric stylisation dictated by local tradition.

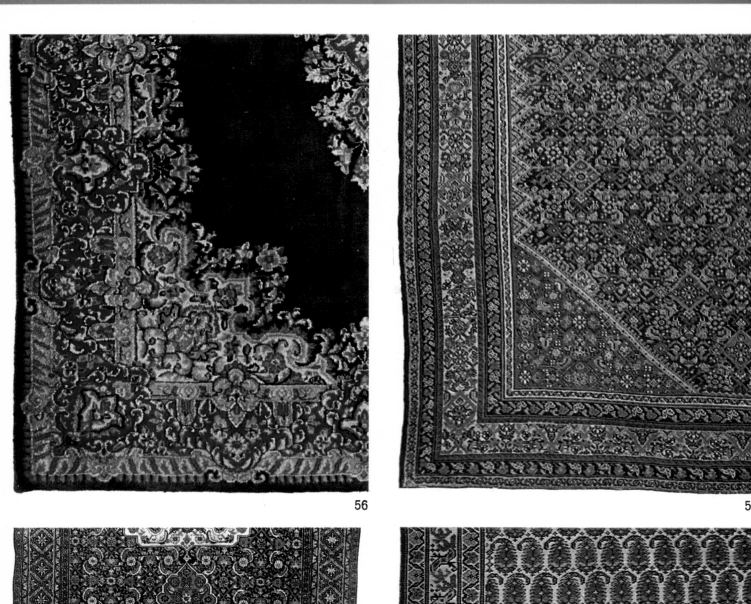

56

57

58

59

60

61

62

This page, the one preceding and those following contain examples of carpets which can be found on sale, and which date from the nineteenth and twentieth centuries. Those shown in plates 56 to 62 are of Persian make.

56 Kerman

57 Feraghan

58 Khurasan

59 Sehna

60 Shiraz

61 Saruk

62 Bijar

63

64

65

66

67

The examples shown on this page, from plates 63 to 67, exemplify types of carpets produced in Asia Minor (Turkey and Anatolia).

63 Ghiordes

64 Ladik

65 Kula

66 Kirsehir

67 Bergama

68

69

70

71

72

73

The examples shown on this page, from plates 68 to 73, exemplify
types of carpets produced in the Caucasus.

68 Kuba

69 Hila

70 Shirvan

71 Chichi

72 Sumak

73 Kazakh

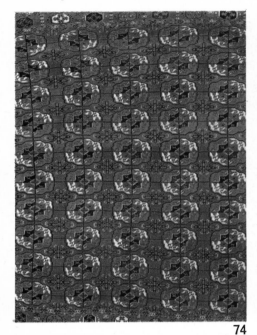

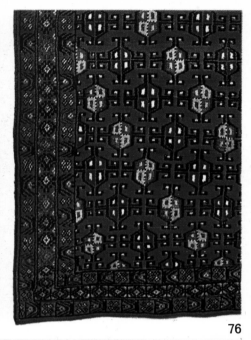

74

75

76

77

78

The examples shown on this page, from plates 74 to 77, exemplify types of carpets produced in Central Asia and generally called Turkestan carpets. The ones shown in plates 78 and 79 come from Chinese Turkestan and are sometimes called Samarkand carpets.

74 Bukhara

75 Yomud

76 Beshir

77 Afghan

78 Kotan

79 Kashgar

79